THE OFFICIAL IRISH JOKE BOOK NO. 3

(BOOK 2 TO FOLLOW)

Also in this series:

Acknowledgments

The Editor wishes to acknowledge the help
and inspiration of a number of people,
particularly Matthew and Nick Cannon,
and Mr. and Mrs. Kettle

Edited by:
Peter Hornby

The Official Irish Joke Book No. 3

(Book 2 to follow)

A Futura Book

First published in Great Britain by
Futura Publications Limited in 1978
Copyright © Futura Publications Limited, 1978
Reprinted 1981, 1982, 1983, 1984 (twice)

ISBN 0 7088 1357 7

Printed in Great Britain by
Hazell Watson & Viney Limited,
Member of the BPCC Group,
Aylesbury, Bucks

Futura Publications
A Division of
Macdonald & Co (Publishers) Ltd
Maxwell House
74 Worship Street
London EC2A 2EN
A BPCC plc Company

Paddy was talking to Mick. 'It's not true dat the English are against us. Why, you can go to London, and if you meet an Englishman, he'll take you home, even share his bed with you, and give you breakfast in the morning, all free.'

'Did that happen to you, den, Paddy?' asked Mick.

'No, but it happened to my sister.'

* * *

Mick, who had been working in England, went back to Ireland, to find his mates, Lenny and Sean were going to Liverpool. 'You'll love England,' he told them. 'Everything's big there – the money's big, the birds are big, the factories are big, and the building sites – WOW!'

Lenny and Sean duly landed in Liverpool and as they walked down the gangplank, Sean saw an anchor lying on the quayside, 'Bejaasus, Lenny, Mick wasn't kidding – look at the size of dat pickaxe dare.'

* * *

Paddy was out digging his garden one day, when he saw a little creature at his feet. He lifted his shovel up to kill it, but to his surprise it spoke. 'Paddy, I'm a leprachaun. Spare my life and I'll grant ye three wishes.'

'Tree wishes. Done,' said Paddy, then thought: 'Well Oi'm tirsty from all dis digging, Oi'd like a bottle o' cold Guinness.' The leprachaun snapped his fingers, and Paddy found he was holding a bottle of Guinness. 'Dat dare,' said the leprachaun, 'is a magic bottle. It'll never empty – it'll pour forever.' Paddy took a swig. Lovely.

'What are your next two wishes, Paddy?' asked the leprachaun. Paddy thought, 'Oi tink Oi'd like two more o dese, please.'

* * *

An Irishman went into the Post Office for six first class stamps. He'd had six letters from his friend and he thought it was time for him to reply to them.

* * *

There's now a serious shortage of ice in Ireland. Murphy died and he took the recipe with him.

* * *

The Irish paratroop trainees were flying out for their first parachute jump, after several weeks training. 'Remember, lads,' said the instructor, 'Yell "Geronimo", jump out, count to eight and then pull your ripcord.'

The door opened at 10,000 feet, all the lads jumped out one by one, and Paddy went last. The instructor shut the door, and the plane flew down and landed. The instructor got out and saw Paddy, frantically clutching the 'plane wing.

'What the hell do you think you're doing?' yelled the instructor.

'Sorry, sorr,' said Paddy, 'but Oi forgot de name of dat bleeding Indian!'

*　　*　　*

A small English soldier wandered into a pub in Ireland one lunchtime. Four I.R.A. men barred his way – 'Get out!!' they said.

There was one hell of a scuffle, which ended with the I.R.A. men unconscious on the floor.

The little soldier walked over to the bar, bought a pint and a pie, walked back, cut the ears off the I.R.A. men, popped them in his pie, and ate it.

'What sort of a soldier are you, Sir?' asked the landlord.

'Pie-and-ear corps,' was the reply.

*　　*　　*

On hearing of an Irish mother who had thirty kids, the Pope sent a cardinal to congratulate her on her achievement. He found his way into the back streets of Dublin and knocked on the door. When the woman answered, the Cardinal delivered his message: 'I'm here to congratulate you on having thirty children. The Pope is very proud of you.'
Mother: 'But I'm Protestant!'
Cardinal: 'What! You filthy sex maniac.'

* * *

Paddy's wife gave birth to triplets – Paddy is now looking for two other men.

* * *

A motorist came to a ford in his travels round Ireland. 'I say,' he said to a passing Irish farmer, 'is the water here deep?'
'No, Sorr,' was the reply.
The motorist drove into the ford, and the water came over the wheels, the bonnet and through the side window. The driver got out of the car and shouted angrily, 'I thought you said the water wasn't deep!'
'Well it only came up to the waist of dem ducks, and dey aren't more dan six inches high!'

* * *

An Irishman opened up a launderette business next door to the local church, after a friend had told him that cleanliness is next to Godliness.

*   *   *

Paddy drove his lorry off Beachy Head to test the air brakes.

*   *   *

Due to a long drought in Ireland, some Irish witches got together and planned to have a rain making ceremony at Mr. O'Donal's Farm, a mile out of Londonderry. If wet, it was to be held in Londonderry Town Hall.

*   *   *

Paddy's Showband was asked to do something typically Irish – so they went up, took the roof off the Theatre and dug up the carpark.

*   *   *

How does an Irishman make love? You don't know? Gosh, I thought only Irishmen were thick.

*   *   *

Tourist to Irish waiter in a Dublin Cafe: 'What are the prawns like today?'
Waiter replied: 'Little pink fishes same as yesterday.'

* * *

Paddy thought that the Pontius Pilot worked for A.E.R. Lingus.

* * *

Then there was the Irish suicide victim. He tried to kill himself by throwing himself off the top of Blackpool tower to the ground. But he missed.

* * *

There is a revised edition of the 'Invisible Man' to be published by a firm of Irish publishers. It is to be illustrated.

* * *

Then there was a group of Irish families on tour to visit one of Britain's most notorious mazes. They spent all day trying to get in.

* * *

Have you heard about the fabulous Antrim String Quartet? It has six members.

* * *

Then there was the one about the Irishman who wanted to be buried at sea. The gravediggers were drowned trying to dig the grave.

* * *

Seeing the sign on the tube ALL DOGS MUST BE CARRIED UP THE ESCALATOR, Paddy spent two hours finding a dog.

* * *

Have you heard about Paddy's obscene phone call? He said, 'You've a lovely voice and you sound very sexy but don't keep telling me the time.'

* * *

Did you hear about the Irish mugger who threatened to beat anybody up if they tried to give him money.

* * *

Paddy thought the lights on his car weren't working, so he asked Mick to stand in front of it to help him.
'Headlights on?'
'Dey are dat, Paddy.'
'Sidelights on?'
'Dey are dat, Paddy.'
'Left indicator?'
'No, Paddy – wait – yes! No – Yes! No . . . !'

* * *

SERGEANT IN ARMY TO IRISH SOLDIER WHO IS LATE FOR DUTY: Do you realize that it is now 16.00 hours, O'Neill?
O'NEILL: No, Serg. Moi watch only goes up to twelve.

*   *   *

Then there was the Irish vampire who went to the blood bank to make a withdrawal.

*   *   *

Did you hear about the Irish Kamakazi pilot? He's writing his memoirs.

*   *   *

When there was a water shortage in Ireland the Irish were going to dilute the water to make it go further.

*   *   *

How do you define 144 Irishmen? Gross Stupidity.

*   *   *

An Irish drug addict tried to smoke pot, but he forgot to take the flowers out.

*   *   *

A thick shepherd had 100 sheep which he counted every morning. One morning he counted as usual ... 96 ... 97 ... 98 ... 99 ... and found he was one short, but thought nothing of it. Next morning he counted as usual ... 96 ... 97 ... 98 ... He was a bit puzzled but shrugged and forgot it.

Next morning, however, when he counted and found he only had 97 sheep left, he thought something should be done. So he rallied all his mates, Paddy, Mick and the others, and they set off to find the thief. They searched hills, valleys, dales, everywhere they could think of, and just as dusk was falling, they saw a shadowy figure on the horizon, carrying a gun over one shoulder and a dead sheep over the other. The shepherd began running towards him, 'Hey, you! Stop Thief! What's that over your shoulder?'

'It's – er – a Winchester .33. Why?'

'No, not that one, the other shoulder!'

'Eugh!! Get off, get off!!'

* * *

Two Irish tramps were not doing very well in life so, as they were walking along the road, they decided to part and go their own ways and then they would meet in two weeks 'time to see if either of them had made any progress. Two weeks later one of them saw the other one driving down the road towards him in a big Rolls-Royce. 'Gosh, where did you get dat big posh car from?' 'Well, just after we parted, Oi got picked up by this lovely young woman driving dis car. She drove me to the nearest woods, and stripped off her clothes and told me to take what I wanted.'

'So, what did you do next?' asked the other tramp.

'Well, as her clothes didn't fit me, Oi took the Rolls instead.'

* * *

Paddy and Mick won £534,645 on their pools syndicate. They went out for a meal to celebrate. What a lovely meal, 7 courses and they had six bottles of wine. Their bill came to £68.35. 'Oi'll pay,' said Mick. They paid up and went on their way to find two women for the night. None of the women seemed to be interested in them, despite all their money. Eventually, they came to a car sales showroom. 'Perhaps we'd get women better if we had a car each,' suggested Mick. So they looked round the showrooms and they both decided on a Rolls-Royce. Paddy said, 'Oi'll pay for deese, Mick, you paid for de dinner.'

* * *

An Irishman won £200 in a raffle, and when a friend asked him two months later what he had done with the money, he said that it had all gone. 'What on earth did you spend it all on?' he asked the Irishman. 'Well, I spent £75 on Guinness, £35 on women, £40 on cigarettes and £25 on gambling,' answered the Irishman. 'Well, that's only £175, what did you do with the other £25?' 'Oh, Oi reckon Oi must have wasted it somewhere.'

* * *

There were four Irish brothers, and one of them died. It had always been his request that he had £500 for a good send off. Two of the brothers refused to donate anything, so the last of them said he would write out a cheque for £500 and put it in the coffin so that he could cash it at the other end.

* * *

Paddy bought a dictionary to read – he said he couldn't follow the story, but at least each word was explained as you went along.

* * *

Do you know the rules of the famous Irish guessing game? One player leaves the room and the others have to guess which one of them has left.

* * *

Did you hear about the Irish Sea Scout? He went camping and his tent sank.

* * *

DO YOU KNOW?

that it takes 100 Irishmen to put a screw in the wall? One to hold the screw – and the other 99 to turn the wall.

*   *   *

how an Irishman calls for his dog? He puts his fingers in his mouth and shouts 'Rover.'

*   *   *

how to confuse an Irishman? Give him 12 spades and then tell him to take his pick.

*   *   *

how you can make an Irishman laugh on Boxing Day? Tell him a joke on Christmas Eve.

*   *   *

how to tell a level-headed Irishman? He dribbles from both sides of his mouth at the same time.

*   *   *

what the fastest game in the world is? Pass the parcel in Belfast.

*   *   *

why Irishmen wear wellies? To keep their brains warm.

*   *   *

what the Irish National Anthem is called? 'Sing Something Simple.'

*   *   *

where the Irish priests are trained? Dymchurch.

*   *   *

how to brainwash an Irishman? Pour Guinness into his wellies.

*   *   *

how to sink an Irish submarine? Tap on the hatch when it's submerged.

*   *   *

the Irish method of finding mines? Place hands firmly over ears, and bang the foot hard down on the ground.

*   *   *

what you would get if you crossed an Irishman with a pig? Thick bacon.

*   *   *

what is black, shrivelled and hangs from a ceiling? An Irish electrician.

*   *   *

DID YOU HEAR ABOUT THE IRISHMAN WHO...

kidnapped the Prime Minister of Ireland and then sent him home with the Ransom Note?

*   *   *

went in the Tunnel of Love at the Fun Fair? He demanded his money back because nobody had loved him.

*   *   *

was taking his driving test? He rolled forward in a hill start.

*   *   *

thought that Sherlock Holmes was a block of Flats?

*   *   *

went to the dentists to have a wisdom tooth put in?

*   *   *

was swimming the Channel? He got tired half way, so he turned back.

*   *   *

was a bricklayer? He applied for a job with Weetabix the Builders.

*   *   *

bought a paper shop? It blew away.

*   *   *

wanted to buy a house? He went to British Home Stores.

*   *   *

went to a Race Meeting at Ascot for the first time? He put 20p each way on a horse and was so disappointed when it only ran one way up the course that he went and demanded his money back.

*   *   *

was bought a pair of water-wings for his birthday? He was killed the same day. He'd jumped from the roof of his house whilst trying to learn to fly when it was raining.

*   *   *

thought that Sheffield Wednesday was a Bank Holiday?

* * *

moved his house three feet to tighten the clothes
line?

* * *

thought that Ellesmere Port was a new type of dinner
wine?

* * *

failed his driving test? He'd opened the door to let
the clutch out.

* * *

was out for a walk one day, and he came across some
milk churns in a field? He thought he'd found a
cow's nest.

* * *

was picking his nose? He tore the lining out of his cap.

*   *   *

Did you hear about the Irish Evel Knievil? He attempted to jump over 32 motor bikes driving a double decker bus.

*   *   *

Seamus O'Neil drove in the Indianapolis 500. He had 32 pit stops — 1 for petrol — 31 to ask the way.

*   *   *

An Irishman has entered for two events in the 1980 Olympic Games — Heading the Shot and Catching the Javelin.

*   *   *

The Irish never worry about the Olympics. They always passed the Dope Tests.

*   *   *

It is the final round in the Olympic diving competition. The atmosphere is incredibly tense as three contestants all share first place. The rabble have all dived, leaving just these three: the American, the Russian and (yes, you've guessed it) the Irishman, to fight it out over the medals. There is absolute silence in the three-quarters of a million pounds new pool as the American steps onto the high board. He takes a sip of barley water and slips out of his towelling gown to reveal the most amazing all-American body; beautifully, Californian sun-bronzed flesh, droopy Mark Spitz moustache, perfectly shaped glistening white teeth, genitals bulging in his tight stars-and-stripes swimming trunks, and oh my God, look at those rippling muscles! He limbers up for a few seconds, clenches his fists in concentration and then springs forward ... What a dive!! Two-and-a-half backward somersaults, a splits and a perfect entry into the water. He swims to the side and casually drags himself out of the water with a smile at the photographers and a wave at the spectators.

Silence. The judges lift up their cards; Technique: 9.8 9.8 9.8 9.8 9.8. The crowd go wild with delight. Appearance: 9.8 9.8 9.8 9.8 9.8. Even more noise. The commentator shouts and screams. Surely the gold must go to the U.S.A.?

Unruffled, the Russian takes a swig of his doped vodka and strides along the board. He is an ox of a man; six feet nine and twenty four inches round the thigh. The crowd hum and finally hush. The Russian dives; a triple backward somersault and a salko. The crowd leap to their feet as one. The commentator swallows his microphone in a frenzy. The judges sit poker faced for a few seconds and then lift their cards; Technique: 9.8 9.8 9.8 9.8 9.8. Appearance: 9.8 9.8 9.8 9.8 9.9. The commentator falls to the floor weeping hysterically. What a day for diving!

So now all eyes are on Mick O'Flaherty, the lowly road digger and part time idiot from Ballyseamus, Donegal. Ladbrokes were offering 5,000,000,000 – 1 on him this morning. Can the impossible happen? He sups his mug of Guinness, shuffles to the edge of the board and without any delay to tense himself to the task with which he is faced, he steps off into the most incredible dive in the history of cosmos. A triple backward somersault and a double salko and splits and a double forward somersault. He hits the water at precisely 90 degrees and leaves it as calm as a millpond. The crowd go absolutely berserk. They sing and shout and jump up and down on each other's stomachs. A small contingent of spectators pick up O'Flaherty and chair him round the pool strewing him with confetti and washing powder.

At last the judges lift their cards. Technique: 10.0 10.0 10.0 10.0 10.0. Fantastic! Amazing! TERRI-FIC! Another roar of acclamation comes from the crowd. The commentator turns blue, stops breathing and has to be carried out. It's just a formality now, but what's this? Appearance: 3.2 4.7 2.2 4.0 3.5. There's an immediate stunned silence and the incredulous Irishman rushes up to the judges' box beside himself with emotion. 'You bastards! I've just done the best bloody dive in the history of the sport and yer bloody well give me two point bloody two.' And picking up the smallest judge by the third rib, he continued, 'Why? Why?' After which he falls to the ground in tears, grovelling at the judges' feet.

'Well, come on,' says the judge, 'just look at you; your donkey jacket's all creased, your wellies are covered in mud . . .'

* * *

Paddy came over to England for a holiday. While there, he went to see a show at which there was one of the best ventriloquists in England. Paddy was so impressed with him that he waited outside the stage door to have a word with the man.

'Oi thought you were great. Oi would very much like you to come and visit me when you are in Ireland. Oi have a big farm, and if you would put on a show for our village, Oi would gladly let you stay at my house, and Oi would see that you had the best of evryting.' The ventriloquist was very flattered, and so the two exchanged addresses and he promised that as soon as he landed in Ireland, he would contact Paddy.

Two months passed and Paddy received a card to say 'Jack the Ventriloquist' was to land at his farm in two days' time. Paddy's wife had the house cleaned from top to bottom, and Paddy had words with all his farm hands to be on their best behaviour.

When the ventriloquist arrived, the first thing Paddy wanted him to do was to get all his animals to say a few words to him. So they walked round the farm and first of all they came to a cow. 'Hello,' said Jack, 'who are you?' 'I am Daisy, the Cow, I have lived here for six years now, and I supply the farmer with milk, and I am very happy here.' 'Dat is brilliant,' said Paddy, 'dat cow has never said a word to me ever before, now how about de horse?'

They walked across the field to where the horse was grazing. 'Hello,' said Jack, 'who are you?' 'I am Neddy, the Horse, I have been here for lots and lots of years, the farmer rides me when he rounds up his sheep, and I am very happy living here.'

'Brilliant,' said Paddy, 'now how about seeing de pigs?'

So they walked over to the pigsties. Jack saw the big

sow on her own in the corner so he went up to her. 'Hello, who are you?' he asked. 'I am Grunter, the pig, I have not lived here very long, when I get fat the farmer will kill me for bacon and ham, but it does not bother me, I get lots to eat so I am very happy.'

Meanwhile, one of the farmhands had been watching the ventriloquist from behind the trees and he had been getting very worried. So he ran to the field in which the sheep were kept, and over to the corner where Fleecy the Ewe was busy eating grass. He got her by the neck. 'Listen 'ere, dares a man coming round 'ere and e'll be asking you a lot of questions, and mention my ——— name, and Oi'll ——— strangle you!!'

*   *   *

Two gay Irishmen – Patrick Fitzwilliam and William Fitzpatrick.

*   *   *

An Irishman complained that the chewing gum he got from the machine in the Gents toilet tasted funny.

*   *   *

Then there was the Irishman who thought that Johnny Cash was the change from a Durex machine.

And the one who thought Muffin the Mule was a sex offence.

*   *   *

Paddy didn't reckon much to sex on the T.V. He kept falling off.

*   *   *

Then there was the Irishwoman who said her husband was unfaithful, because she knew for certain that he wasn't the father of one of her children.

*   *   *

Irishwoman on the telephone: 'Well, if you're the wrong number, then why did you answer the telephone?'

*   *   *

What do you call a pregnant Irishwoman? A dope carrier.

*   *   *

An Irish girl was explaining to her doctor how she got a headache from using cosmetics. She had been putting toilet water on her neck and the seat had fallen onto her.

*   *   *

An Irishwoman complained to her doctor that the contraceptive pill kept dropping out.

* * *

An Irishman took a box of dud matches back to the shop. 'Sorry, sir,' said the assistant, 'but don't you remember testing them before you left the shop?'

* * *

Mick and his wife went looking for two new beds for their children. While the salesman was showing them round the bed department, he pointed out some twin beds that were on special offer. 'Dare no good,' said Mick, 'we've got a daughter who's eight, and a son who's six, we have no twins.'

* * *

An Irishman bought a pair of wellies and took them back two days later for a longer piece of string.

* * *

Then there was the Irishman who took his new tie back to the shop, because it was too tight for him.

* * *

Did you hear about the Irishwoman who bought a colander? She took it back because it had holes in it.

* * *

An Irishman went into a newsagent's shop for a piece of wrapping paper 2 in. x 100 yds., so that he could send a new clothes line to his mother.

*   *   *

His mother sent back the washing line because the garden was not long enough.

.

*   *   *

Paddy bought a new fish shop in England, and on the first night he opened at 7.30 pm. His first customer was an Englishman. 'Fish and chips twice, please.' 'All right, all right,' said Paddy, 'I heard you de first time.'

*   *   *

At a local factory, an extension was being built, one of the labourers just happened to be an Irishman. One day the Irishman went to wash down his wellies before going home, and he used one of the hosepipes on the wall. Five minutes later, the fire engines arrived. The Irishman had used one of the fire hoses to wash his wellies, which had automatically started off the alarm at the local fire station.

*   *   *

And yet another Irishman started work on a building site. The foreman asked him, 'Will you dig me a hole 2oft. deep by 1ooft. long by 4oft. wide today, please?' 'Oi can't do dat in a day, it'll kill me,' said the Irishman. 'We'll give you a J.C.B.' 'Keep your bloody medals, Oi still can't do dat in a day ! !'

*   *   *

On a building site there was an Irishman wearing only one welly. He was working 1ft. in water.

*   *   *

An Irishman was working on a building site. The foreman told him to dig a large hole, and quite deep too. Paddy dug away all day at the hole until it was big enough.
'What shall Oi do with dat spare soil?' he asked the foreman.
'Dig another hole to put it in,' was the answer.

*   *   *

In the year 2001 the inhabitants of the moon begged the United States not to send any more Irish astronauts. Said the senior Moon Man, 'We thought Green Cheese smelled bad until we smelled Irish wellies.'

*   *   *

An Irishman went for a job at a building site. The foreman told him, 'You can start at 7.30 am on Monday morning.' Paddy went back to his flat and told his mates, 'You must get me up at 7.00 am on Monday morning, because Oi start me new job at 7.30 am and Oi mustn't be late on the first morning.' Monday morning arrived and before his mates woke him up, they painted his hands and his face black. 'Paddy, get up it's 7.00 am.' He woke up, had his breakfast and walked across the town to the building site. The foreman went over to him. 'Yes, what can I do for you?' The Irishman said, 'You gave me a job and told me to start this morning.' 'I'm sorry, sir, there must be some mistake, I've only got one man starting this morning, and he's Irish.'
The Irishman left the building site and walked home slowly, as he walked past a shop window, he turned and saw his face black. 'Be Jaasus, dave woke de wrong bloody man up! !'

* * *

Doctor: Now remember, Paddy, just add one teaspoonful of medicine to your Guinness.'
Paddy: Er, would dat be heaped or level, doctor?

* * *

Paddy got a job as a doctor. After his first surgery was nearly over, he got a patient in complaining of regular stomach pains. 'Go home and take two of these tablets about an hour before you feel the pain coming on.'

* * *

An Irishman went to the doctor's with an injured ear and burns on his feet. 'What on earth have you been doing?' asked the doctor. 'Well Oi bought this tinned pudding, doctor, and Oi just did as the instructions said – pierce here and stand in boiling water.'

* * *

An Irish genius has just invented a cure for which there is no known illness.

* * *

Did you hear about the Irish fish? It drowned! !

* * *

Did you hear about the Irish Humpty Dumpty? The wall fell on top of him! !

* * *

It was a peaceful scene in a little pub in Dublin. The customers were sat around playing cards and dominoes, and a dog was quietly chewing a bone in the corner. Then his master stood up and yelled 'Rover!' The dog stood up, wagging his tail, and his hind leg dropped off.

* * *

Did you hear about the Irish tadpole? It turned into a butterfly!!

* * *

Earlier today, a body was found in Armagh with 15 bullets in it, 17 stab wounds, and a rope around its neck. Irish police have ruled out foul play.

* * *

Thieves broke into the library of an Irish Professor, and stole two of the Professor's most valued books. 'The thing that upsets me the most,' said the Professor, 'is that I hadn't finished colouring in one of them.'

* * *

Another Irish forger was very pleased with himself. He'd just discovered that he could file the edges off 50p pieces and he got 10p pieces that would fit into the slot machines in his local.

* * *

The Irish Police Force nearly caught up with one of their most wanted criminals, when they were tipped off that he was at the local cinema. They sealed all exits but, apparently, he had managed to escape through one of the entrances.

* * *

Two Irish terrorists were on their way to plant a bomb. On the way they had to drive up a very bumpy road. 'Go steady, Terry,' said Mick, 'we don't want de bomb to explode.'
'Stop worrying, Mick, if it goes off, dares a spare in de boot.'

* * *

Two Irishmen were sent to prison for twelve years. By the time the twelve years were up, the two mates had perfected a way of communicating with each other. They banged their tin mugs on the radiators to send vibrations along the pipes. Very clever, you might think, but they were in the same cell.

* * *

Paddy stole a calendar – he got twelve months.

* * *

Paddy and his two friends, an Englishman and a Scotsman, got sentenced to 5 years in jail, but were told that they could have one thing with them that they badly wanted. The Englishman had a big blonde, the Scotsman had bottles and bottles of whisky, and Paddy chose packets and packets of cigarettes. Five years came and they were all let out, one by one, the Englishman came out with his blonde looking absolutely knackered, the Scotsman came out staggering all over, and hiccuping, and last of all, out came Paddy, of course – looking very frustrated, and do you know what his first words were? ' 'Ave you got a light, anybody?'

*　　*　　*

Paddy got stopped by the police for speeding up the A1. 'No, officer, Oi wasn't speeding, but Oi've just passed three idiots back there who were.'

*　　*　　*

Two Irishmen were up in court for arson. Dave O'Reilly said he was from no fixed abode, and his friend Patrick said, 'and Oi lives in the flat above him.'

*　　*　　*

There was the Irishman who cut himself badly during a smash and grab raid. He forgot to let go of the brick.

*   *   *

Then there was the Irishman who was up in court and was found guilty of trying to gas his wife by throwing her into the North Sea.

*   *   *

And in the same court, another Irishman was found not guilty on a charge of indecency. He'd streaked through a nudist camp.

*   *   *

Did you hear about the Irish forger? The police broke into his house and took away half a million nine pound notes.

*   *   *

An Irishman was killed when a bullet missed his ear by 2 inches. It got him in the forehead.

*   *   *

Do you know how they play Irish roulette? Same as Russian, but with a bullet in every chamber.

*   *   *

Did you hear about the Irish Firing Squad? They formed a circle.

*   *   *

Paddy was staying as a guest on an English farm, and was feeling rather bored. 'Now I'm busy at the moment, but if you want to amuse yourself for an hour or so, take my gun and two gun dogs and go and do some shooting and I will be free soon,' said the farmer. Five minutes later, Paddy was back again. 'Have you got any more gun dogs, Sorr?'

*   *   *

Q. How can you tell when an Irishman is getting over his illness?
A. He tries to blow the foam off his medicine.

*   *   *

Two Irishmen, Paddy and Mick came to live in London. After a couple of months in London, and they still hadn't found jobs, they made big plans for a Bank Robbery. But they then decide between them that everyone would easily recognize their accents, and they would easily be found. After a bit more thought they came to the conclusion that the best thing to do would be to acquire a nice proper English accent by attending elocution classes.

Six months went by and they finished elocution classes, having both acquired very well spoken and very English accents. Their next step was to make an appointment with the Bank Manager and wait until the great day arrived.

'Oh, Good Afternoon, Sir,' they both said together as they made themselves comfortable in the easy chairs in the Manager's office. 'Now, I hope you are going to co-operate, Sir, we need £50,000 in rather a rush,' said Mick, 'and just in case you don't intend to be very co-operative, my friend here has got a sawn-off shotgun under his coat (Paddy is by now revealing the gun from under his coat), which we will use should you not . . .'

'Excuse me for interrupting, Sir, but are you two by any chance Irishmen?' asked the Bank Manager.

'Well, Oi have to be honest with you dare, Sorr, yes, we are Irish, but how on eart' did you know dat?'

'Well, it's just that you've sawn the wrong bloody end off the shotgun!'

* * *

EXPLORER: ... and up the Amazon, at midnight the temperature was 126°F.
PADDY: Er, would dat be in de shade?

* * *

An Irishman phoned Heathrow Airport wanting to know approximately how long a flight to New York would take. 'Just a minute,' said the girl, who was very busy. 'Oi'm very grateful to you, tanks very much,' said Paddy, and then hung up.

* * *

An Irishman steps onto a P.A.Y.E. bus in England. He wonders what the driver is holding out his hand for, but nevertheless, he says, 'Oi'll pay you when Oi gets some change from de conductress.'

* * *

Did you hear about the Irishman who was stranded on a desert island for two years? An empty life boat floated up to his island so he knocked it to bits and made himself a raft.

* * *

PADDY: (TO TICKET MAN AT KING'S CROSS STATION) Could Oi have a return ticket, please?
TICKET MAN: Yes, Sir, where to please?
PADDY: Well, back here of course, you fool!

* * *

Paddy told his friend, 'Oi've put one over on British Rail – Oi've bought a return ticket to Dublin and Oi'm not coming back!'

*　*　*

Two Irish boys were travelling down to London on their motor-bikes. Seamus had not been before and Tommy had. Seamus said to Tommy, 'Seeing as you know the way and I don't, Tommy, you go on ahead and I will follow on in front.'

*　*　*

Patrick O'Columbus sailed to discover America but he fell off the edge.

*　*　*

There was to be a launching of an Irish moon rocket, but it had to be postponed because they couldn't find a bottle big enough to take the stick.

*　*　*

An Irishman was sent to the sun in a rocket. He blasted off at night to avoid the heat.

*　*　*

How do you know which is the Captain of an Aer Lingus plane? He has gold braid round his wellies.

*   *   *

Then there was the Irish jet pilot who refused to go in the jet until they'd put the propeller back on.

*   *   *

Two Irishmen were parachuting into the desert in Egypt during the night to begin a job for the Arabs the next morning. As it began to get lighter, and the Irishmen saw all the sand around them, one said to the other, 'Bloody 'ell, let's get out of here now, Patrick, before de cement arrives.'

*   *   *

Paddy got a job working as a Slot Meter Collector for the Electricity Board. Before he went out on his first morning's work, he was told by the foreman, 'And don't forget to come in for your pay at 4.00 pm on Thursday nights.'
'BE JAASUS,' said Paddy, 'DO WE GET PAID AS WELL?'

*   *   *

An Irishman went to Canada for a job as a lumber-jack. Whilst he was walking through the forests, he came across two men using a cross-cut saw. A big man was pulling at one end, and then a little man was pulling at the other end. The Irishman stood and watched for a while and then he went up to the big man, with his fists clenched. 'Now listen 'ere,' he said, 'if de little man wants to use de saw, let him have it, before Oi knock yer 'ead in.'

* * *

There was the Irishman who applied for a job at his local Grand Hotel. 'You've got the job,' said the Manager, 'but first will you fill me in a question-naire, please?' So Paddy went and beat up the door-man.

* * *

A Paddy recently moved to the country and bought a chicken ranch, then discovered that all his chickens were laying sterile eggs. So he bought himself a shot-gun, pushed the rooster up against the henhouse wall and demanded to know where he was hiding the condoms.

* * *

Paddy emigrated to Canada, and applied for a job as a lumberjack. He was told by the foreman, 'All my men cut 100 or more trees down every day, we will give you a day's trial to see how you can cope.' He gave Paddy an electric saw and left him to it, saying that he would be back at 5.00 to see how he had gone on.

At 5 o'clock the foreman was back, he counted up the trees – 98. 'Sorry, Paddy, but it won't do, it must be a hundred.' 'Well, Sorr,' said Paddy, 'Oi'm just getting into the hang of it, Oi haven't worked for two years, but Oi swear blind Oi will make a hundred tomorrow.' 'O.K., Paddy, I will give you another chance, seeing as most of the men said that you haven't stopped for a rest all day; you seem to be a hard-working lad.'

The next day at 5 o'clock the foreman was back again – 99 trees this time. He liked Paddy, a nice quiet lad, not like some he could name. He thought 98, 99, he's bound to do a hundred tomorrow. 'I'll give you one more day's trial, Paddy.'

It was soon 5 o'clock again, the foreman was round again, counting the trees – 99.

'Sorry, Paddy, you're finished.' Paddy picked up his things and started to walk away, head down, looking glum. The foreman felt a touch of sympathy. 'Just a minute, Paddy, I think I'll check your saw first, it could be a bit blunt.' He picked up the saw, inspected it for a minute, then he pressed the button and started the saw up.

'BE JAASUS!!' shouted Paddy. 'WHAT DE BLOODY 'ELL IS DAT NOISE???'

* * *

An Irishman had been living in England for a year or so and he thought it was time he wrote a letter to his mother.

Dear Mother,
Sorry I haven't written to you for a long time, but I have been very busy. I have a good job at the local biscuit factory. I get a good wage. I have a nice flat. I don't have an electricity bill, so I save a lot of money there. But there is a slot machine in the flat, and I seem to put a lot of money into that and watching to see if the numbers come up. I never win anything though. There is a man who comes round to empty it and he gives me a bit of money back. I think it must be what should have dropped out of the machine when I have won. Still, you'd think that if it was faulty he'd fix it, wouldn't you, after all, I might have won more than he's been giving me back, or he might be giving me too much back . . .

*　　*　　*

WHAT DO YOU CALL?
What do you call an Irish Frankenstein?
'BEGORRAH.'

*　　*　　*

What do you call an Irishman with half a brain?
GIFTED!

*　　*　　*

What do you call an Irish Canadian with antlers?
MICKEY MOOSE.

*　　*　　*

What do you call an Irishman wearing a balaclava?
Anything you like, he won't hear you.

*　　*　　*

What do you call an Irishman on a bike? A dope
peddlar.

*　　*　　*

What do you call an Irish Brain Surgeon? A Chiro-
podist.

*　　*　　*

What do you call an Irishman with a degree? A
LIAR!!

*　　*　　*

Murphy is a wonderful husband and a most unusual
Irishman. Unlike his brothers and cousins, he doesn't
guzzle Guinness, gamble, snore, wipe his nose on his
shirt sleeve. And you should see the groovy things he
makes with his own two hands. Why he even makes
his own dresses!

*　　*　　*

Patrick O'Flynn was studying Greek Mythology. When asked what was half beast and half man, he replied, 'Could it be Buffalo Bill?'

*   *   *

Paddy was on University Challenge. When asked 'Where are the Andes?' Paddy replied, 'On the end of my Wristies.'
Asked what was Ghandi's first name – Replied, 'Could it be Goosey, Goosey?'
Asked what are Hippies – Replied, 'Could it be to hang your leggies on?'

*   *   *

PADDY WAS ON MASTERMIND

Magnus Magnusson: What's your name?
Paddy: Pass ...
M.M. : What's the first letter of the alphabet?
Paddy: Eh?
M.M. : Correct. Who invented the steam engine?
Paddy: What?
M.M. : Quite right. Now here's a difficult one. What is the correct term for a person who eats other humans?
(Paddy keeps quiet. Can't think of the answer)
M.M. : I can see you're having trouble. Can't you have a try?
Paddy: Ah canna. Balls!
M.M. : Well done, sir!

*   *   *

THE IRISH G.C.E. 'O' LEVEL PAPER

PART A

A1. Who won the second world war? Who was second?

A2. What is a silver dollar made of?

A3. Explain Einstein's theory of Hydrodynamics or write your name in block capital letters.

A4. Spell the following: Dog – Cat – Fish.

A5. What time is News at Ten on?

A6. Approximately how many commandments was Moses given? (State whether you just guessed.)

A7. There have been six kings of England called George, one called George the First, name the other five.

A8. Write down the numbers 1 – 10. (Marks will be deducted for every number out of sequence.)

A9. Who invented Stephenson's Rocket?

A10. What musical instrument does Phil the Fluter play?

A11. What colour is a red London bus?

* * *

PART B

B1. Do you understand Newton's Law of Gravity? (answer Yes or No.)

B2. Spot the deliberate mistake: AN APPLE A DAY GATHERS NO MOSS.

B3. Name the odd man out: SHEMUS O'TOOLE, JEAN O'FLATTERY, PATRICK MURPHY, MAHATMA GHANDI.

B4. Name the odd man out: CARDINAL HEENAN, THE POPE, THE ARCHBISHOP OF CANTERBURY, JACK THE RIPPER.

B5. Is a dunker (a) A person who dips his biscuits in his tea?
(b) A contraceptive?
(c) A lorry for Motorway construction?

B6. Name the winning jockey of the 1975 Greyhound Derby.

B7. Who built the Pyramids (McAlpine, Wimpeys, Pharaohs, Tysons, or still out for tender).

B8. In the 1972 Irish Sheepdog Trials, how many dogs were found guilty?

B9. Write down all you know in not less than three words.

B10. Write down your name. (Candidates are advised not to copy.)

B11. Anyone found copying all other questions will be awarded double.

B12. Where were the survivors of the Great Fire of London buried?

*　　*　　*

During World War I an Irish infantryman from Co. Tipperary wrote to his wife that he had been seriously wounded in the Dardanelles.
Her reply was succinct: 'Does that mean that we can't have any more children?'

*　　*　　*

For some reason three Irishmen were sent to measure the height of a flagpole. For hours they kept jumping up and down, falling off ladders and getting nowhere until a passing Irishman told them the metal pole could be unscrewed from its base and laid on the grass.

'Listen, you stupid mick,' one of the Irishmen said. 'We were sent out here to measure the height of the pole – not its length.'

*   *   *

Of all the western nations Ireland is unique in that it has no income tax. The reason is simple – it has no income.

*   *   *

An Irishman in Dublin went to the local civil service headquarters to apply for a job.

'What can you do? he was asked by the personnel chief.

'Nothing,' he answered.

'That's good,' he was told. 'Now we won't have to break you in.'

*   *   *

What do you call an I.R.A. man with a submachine-gun? SIR! !.

*   *   *

A concerned clergyman rushed into a police station to report a dead donkey lying outside in the street. Wanting to make his little joke for the day, the Irish sergeant said, 'That's hardly your business, is it, father?'

'Sure it is,' the irritated padre said, 'I had to notify the next of kin.'

* * *

'Can you make a Martini?' the restaurant owner asked the would-be Irish barmaid.

'No,' she answered, 'I don't put out for wops.'

* * *

Asked why she thought she was bionic, the Irish girl explained that she had been made by a scientist.

* * *

It was raining like hell and young Murphy was preparing to go out on a very special date.

'Listen, son,' his mother warned, 'don't you go out without your rubbers on a night like this.'

'That's okay, Ma,' he replied, 'I got three of them right here in my wallet.'

* * *

An Irish couple adopted a war orphan and decided to learn Vietnamese so they'd understand what the baby was saying when it grew up.

*　　*　　*

Did you hear about the Irishman who was asked by the psychiatrist if he stirred his tea with his left or right hand.
'Neither,' said Paddy, 'I usually use a spoon.'

*　　*　　*

'Listen, Michael,' said the school teacher, 'you know you can't sleep in my class.'
'That's the trouble with it,' he said. 'Why do you have to talk so loud all the time?'

*　　*　　*

'When I serve dinner should I say, "Dinner is ready" or "Dinner is served"?' the new Irish cook asked her mistress.
'If you cook it the way you cooked it yesterday, just say, "Dinner is ruined," ' said the lady of the house.

*　　*　　*

Staring at a painting of a huge nude woman in a museum, the Irish art critic said dreamily, 'Now there's something I could really get my teeth in to.'

*　　*　　*

Q. Why are so many Irish wives angry and dissatisfied?
A. Because they're married to Irishmen.

* * *

Another Irishman was working on a building site. The foreman said to him, 'Go and fetch me that wheelbarrow over there!' When the Irishman came back, he was wheeling one wheelbarrow with another one inside it. 'I only wanted one,' said the foreman. 'Oi know, but you didn't expect me to carry it, did you?'

* * *

'Fingers' O'Shaunnassey is the most celebrated cracksman in the Dublin underworld because he has finally learned how to pick the locks of pay toilets.

* * *

It was easy for Will Rogers to say he never met a man he didn't like. He didn't know any Irishmen.

* * *

'SILENCE IN THE LIBRARY,' the Irish scholar said loudly.

* * *

'If Henry Ford and Gerald Ford aren't the same person, how come you don't ever see them together?' the intelligent Irishman wanted to know at a political gathering.

* * *

One of the reasons so few Irishmen go back to Ireland is that they don't know exactly where it is.

* * *

Q. If all the generals in the Irish Army pooled their brains, what would you come up with?
A. A private first class with a low IQ.

* * *

Told that he ought to join a mass demonstration to protest the proliferation of the Official Irish Joke Book, lazy Paddy said, 'I don't care what they call me as long as they don't call me late for lunch.'

* * *

Q. Why was the recent Irish H-Bomb test such a total failure?
A. Somebody forgot to bring along a match to light the fuse.

* * *

Q. Why are there so few Irish criminals in the United States?
A. Well, you know, it takes some brains to be a crook.

*   *   *

Q. India has its Untouchables, that great mass of scurvy, unwanted citizens despised by the rest of the populace. What does America have?
A. The Irish.

*   *   *

In Ireland an institution of higher learning is any grade school with a second floor.

*   *   *

If it's true that 'cleanliness is next to Godliness', then it's no wonder that so many Paddys go to Hell.

*   *   *

In most British restaurants they feature 'soup of the day' on the menu. In Irish restaurants they call it 'soup of the month'. Quite simply because it takes them that long to make up their minds.

*   *   *

In Ireland a rock festival is where they stone the band to death if they don't like the music.

*   *   *

Contrary to what most people think, the expression 'Never trust anyone over 30' was coined by an Irishman rather than by an American. The reason is simple – the Irish could only count to 29.

*   *   *

Unlike blacks, Irishmen don't have a natural sense of rhythm. In fact, they don't have any kind of sense.

*   *   *

An Irish loser is a man who doesn't have enough busfare to get down to Social Services to sign up for welfare.

*   *   *

Q. Why were Irish so popular during the great Oklahoma land rush?
A. Because they were the only ones strong enough to pull the wagons after the horses died.

*   *   *

Q. Name the three most famous Irishmen of all time.
A.   and we can't remember the name of the other guy.

*   *   *

'I want a hundred pounds a week to start,' the Irish typist told the personnel manager of a large company.
'I'll pay you that with pleasure,' the man said.
Sniffed the not so bright lady, 'With pleasure, I'll expect to be paid a hundred and fifty.'

* * *

'Ya think ya got it tough,' O'Reilly's wife yelled at her Paddy during a drunken Saturday night brawl when the beer bottles were flying like shrapnel. 'Well, I'm the one that's got it hard. Me sweating all day over a hot stove while you're down there in a nice cool sewer.'

* * *

Irishman passes a newspaper shop. He sees headlines on the newsboard '300 JOBS IN JEOPARDY'. He rushes to the nearest railway station. 'Could Oi 'ave a ticket to Jeopardy, please?'

* * *

'What's the matter?' Casey asked his wife. 'You only talked twenty minutes on the phone.'
'I know,' agreed the wife. 'I got a wrong number.'

* * *

And then, of course, there is the Irishman who thinks Sydney Australia is just one more rock star.

* * *

And then there was the Irish colleen who was so ugly that Peeping Toms would call her on the telephone and beg her to pull the curtains.

* * *

Two Irish tramps had pooled their savings to buy a quart of whiskey and now lay blissfully drunk in a filthy doss house. 'Man, I feel great,' the first tramp said. 'I wouldn't trade how I feel for a million pounds.'
'Then what about ten million?' his friend asked.
'Not nearly enough,' was the answer.
'Okay, suppose somebody offered you twenty million?'
'I guess I'd have to think about it,' said the first tramp, 'because now you're talking about real money.'

* * *

Q. How can you tell when Murphy is really drunk?
A. When he tries to take his pants off over his head.

* * *

'My son plays the piano just like the finest piano virtuoso in the land,' the Irishman rather proudly informed the sceptical booking agent in London.

*   *   *

'Listen here, Shaun,' the girl's father asked, sizing up the suitor, 'do you really think you could provide for my daughter on, say, a hundred pounds a week?'
'I think I could,' said Shaun, 'if that's the best offer you can make.'

*   *   *

'Hey, man, I'm glad to see you,' Patrick told his old pal Michael. 'There's a rumour going round that you're dead.'
'I heard that rumour myself,' Patrick answered, 'but when I checked it out I discovered it was some other guy.'

*   *   *

The lady of the manor warned the Irish mover to be extra careful with a Chinese vase because it was five thousand years old. Said the Irishman, 'I'll be just as careful with it as if it was new.'

*   *   *

Terry and Mick were sat in their digs one night, Mick was doing a crossword, and Terry was watching the television. 'Terry, Oi'm stuck with one 'o dese clues, four letters, Old MacDonald had one.' 'Dat's easy, Mick – farm,' said Terry. 'How do you spell dat?' 'Ummm – E.I.E.I.O.'

* * *

Murphy, the Dublin clown, thought he'd have some fun with native New Yorkers who are supposed to be the biggest suckers alive. But the laugh turned out to be on Murphy. The first guy he tried to sell the Brooklyn Bridge to actually owned the damned thing – and our Irish friend had to give him twenty dollars or he would have called the police.

* * *

'What's the idea of coming in here with mud smeared all over your shoes?' the restaurant manager yelled at the Irishman just in town from the country. 'What shoes?' the Irishman wanted to know.

* * *

One of the most famous murder mysteries in the world is the one where the butler didn't do it. Why not? Because he was Irish – and therefore too stupid.

* * *

Walking home from the unemployment office where he had just picked up his weekly cheque, Murphy ran into his mother-in-law. 'Last night I dreamed I'd finally found a job,' he told the sour-faced lady.
'No wonder you look so tired,' she said acidly.

*　　*　　*

Did you ever hear about Murphy with the worst case of insomnia in all of Dublin. Every twenty-four hours he'd wake up and couldn't go back to sleep for at least twenty minutes.

*　　*　　*

A dedicated reader of statistical tables in almanacs, Paddy told his favourite barman, 'Every time I breathe in and out somebody dies somewhere in the world. Isn't that amazing?'
'It wouldn't be if you tried using a mouthwash,' the bored mixologist replied.

*　　*　　*

Two Irish drunks were sitting at a bar in Dublin. One turned to the other and asked,
'You know what time it is?'
'That I do,' said the second.
'Thanks.'

*　　*　　*

Jean Murphy used to be a run-of-the-gin-mill prostitute. Recently, though, her income seems to have doubled. Asked to explain, said, 'I found a better paying position.'

*　　*　　*

Crying as if her poor old heart would break an old Irish lady approached a policeman and said her dog Fido had been lost. Said the policeman: 'Why don't you put an ad in the papers?'
'I thought of that,' the lady said, 'but then I remembered that dear little Fido can't read.'

*　　*　　*

Angry psychiatrist at an IQ testing institute, 'Murphy, would you mind telling me how it's possible for anyone to be so utterly stupid?'
'It's easy, doc,' said Murphy – 'I'm Irish.'

*　　*　　*

Q. What is the national animal of Ireland?
A. The hyena.

*　　*　　*

Back in the early 19th century, two Irish explorers were hacking their way through the African jungle when they spotted a strange looking animal with a horn on its nose.

'Why don't we call it a rhinoceros?' Paddy asked.

'Why?' came the response.

'Because it looks more like a rhinoceros than anything we've seen so far.'

*　　*　　*

An imaginative but stupid Irish businessman decided to set fire to his failing pub and collect the insurance. So after he'd soaked the place with petrol and set it ablaze, he called the police and told them a wild tale about a frenzied gorilla having done the deed.

Taken down to the police station he repeated his wild story.

'Listen,' said one of the policemen, 'that animal you've been describing sounds more like a baboon than a gorilla. Make up your mind which it's going to be.'

'How can I be sure?' said Paddy. 'He was wearing a mask at the time.'

*　　*　　*

And then there was the Irishman who was so conceited that every time he had a birthday he sent his mother a letter of congratulations.

*　　*　　*

'Define the word taxidermist,' the teacher asked Paddy.

'I don't know,' was the answer.

'Well, it's a man who mounts animals,' the teacher explained.

'That's not what we'd call him in Ireland,' Paddy replied.

*   *   *

And then there is the eminent Irish physician who declares that if a man drinks a cup of hot water for 36,500 mornings he will live to be 100 years old.

*   *   *

'This clock I won at bingo is really super,' Murphy told a friend. 'It can do an hour in forty-five minutes.'

*   *   *

Everyone in Cork C. is talking about Mrs. Murphy's dedication to free enterprise. Recently she bought a bicycle and since then she's been peddling it all over town.

*   *   *

Murphy's sky diver's parachute failed to open and he plunged five thousand feet to his death. A coroner's jury decided that the cause of death was 'Jumping to a conclusion.'

*   *   *

For weeks the newly rich Murphy had been wining and dining the gorgeous American girl without success. He had showered her with love letters and expensive gifts and still she wanted no part of him.

Frustrated and angry, Murphy said to her, 'Let's be honest, honey. What would it take to get you into bed?'

'I'm not sure,' she answered. 'Probably three of your tough friends – and a bottle of chloroform.'

* * *

'Are you ever unfaithful to your wife?' the psychoanalyst asked Paddy.

'Well, sure I am, doc – who else would I be unfaithful to?'

* * *

'How did you get that mink coat?' one Irish girl asked another.

'By struggling hard for years.'

'My advice is – stop struggling and you'll get another in no time.'

* * *

Murphy, always looking to get something for nothing, proudly told a friend that he had managed to furnish one whole room in his new house simply by collecting cigarette coupons.

'But what about all the other rooms?' he was asked.

'They're all filled up with cigarettes,' he admitted.

*　　*　　*

In Irish business circles a Yes Man is a junior executive who always carries a tube of vaseline in his briefcase in case the chairman of the board feels like staying after work.

*　　*　　*

After overtaking a Paddy speeding the policeman said, 'You were doing ninety-five miles an hour. What's the big idea?'

'Well, you see, officer,' said Paddy, 'my brakes just failed back there and I was rushing home before I caused an accident.'

*　　*　　*

'I think it's crazy to let this man charge us twenty pounds just to tow us to a service station,' Murphy's wife said indignantly.

Grinning like a monkey, he said, 'The laugh's on him – I got the handbrake on.'

*　　*　　*

'I drink a pint of Paddy's every night for my insomnia,' O'Reilly said.
'Has it helped?'
'No, but now I don't mind staying awake so much.'

*   *   *

And then there was the Irish taxi driver who was so lazy that he used bumps in the street to knock the ashes off his cigar.

*   *   *

The very young Irish husband who had married a twice-widowed lady wandered into a local candy store and was told by the owner that he would have to pay fifteen cents for an all-day sucker.
'Doesn't seem like much, does it?' he commented.
One of the card-players in the back of the store called out, 'That's what everybody says about your old lady.'

*   *   *

'That's a very loyal dog you have there,' the travelling salesman told the Irish barber in a small town in Co. Cork. 'He stays so close to you while you're cutting your customers' hair.'
'Not true!' said Mick. 'It's just that now and then I snip off a piece of an ear.'

*   *   *

In Ireland O'Reilly married a window dresser and then sued for divorce because she took all the shades out of the bedroom.

* * *

Told by the marriage counsellor that he should engage in sexual foreplay in an effort to save his weary marriage, Paddy (a poor speller) brought three of his friends into the bedroom on that very same night.

* * *

Teaching an Irishman to drive is the quickest way to lose control of your automobile.

* * *

'How long does it take to get from here to the train station?' the would-be home owner asked the Irish estate agent.
'About a ten minute walk, if you run like crazy,' was the reply.

* * *

Old Irish proverb: you can lead an Irishman to water, but you can't make him take a bath.

* * *

Many an Irishman who starts off with the bottle winds up in the jug.

*   *   *

Q. What is more stupid than a stupid Irishman?
A. Nothing – absolutely nothing!

*   *   *

Q. Why did Columbus sail for many months across an unknown ocean with little food and a mutinous crew?
A. He was trying to find a continent where there was no Irishmen.

*   *   *

Q. Why has history neglected to record the fact that there were a dozen Irishmen at the Battle of the Little Big Horn?
A. Actually, they had rather a rotten job – digging all those latrines for the 5,000 Sioux.

*   *   *

Q. Why did the African dictator, recently a cannibal chief, send his secret agents to Dublin to kidnap a famous, pint-sized actor?
A. Because he felt like a little Irish ham.

*   *   *

Q. Why did the Makers of the Declaration of Independence put an asterisk next to the famous phrase – 'All men are created equal?'
A. At the bottom of the page they added – 'All men created equal except Irishmen.'

* * *

'I want you to keep the suspect under constant surveillance,' the Chief of Detectives told the new Irish plainclothes man.
'Got you, Chief,' the Irishman said. 'And I'll keep an eye on him too.'

* * *

Q. If the dog is man's best friend, then what is man's worst enemy?
A. Probably the Irish.

* * *

Q. Why do the Irish find it so hard to read?
A. Because they have never learned to move their lips properly.

* * *

'Just what do you think you're doing?' the first mate asked an Irish sailor on a tramp steamer.
'I'm writing a letter to my old lady.'
'But you know you can't write.'
'That's okay, sir,' Paddy explained. 'My old lady can't read.'

* * *

Q. Why will there never be a New York Times of Ireland?
A. Because none of the news in Ireland is fit to print.

* * *

Q. What is considered to be a big night in a Dublin neighbourhood?
A. Watching the overloaded machines break down in the local laundromat.

* * *

Angered by the fact that his lovely wife had left him for a poet, the hulking Irishman decided to pen some romantic lines in an effort to win her back.
So he wrote the following:
I love my wife,
I love her in her nighty
When the moonlight flits
Across her tits
— Oh Jesus Christ Almighty.

* * *

'Damn it, my good man, this soup is stone cold,' the diner in a fancy restaurant told the Irish waiter. 'Bring me some hot soup right away.'
With a look of great indignation, Paddy replied: 'What are you trying to do, sir? Make me burn my thumb?'

*　　*　　*

The rich and romantic Paddy had long been in love with the lady from the wrong side of the tracks. He knew she had a 'past' but didn't care about it. So – after a long and determined courtship – they were finally married. He took his bride back to his mansion on the hill and there was a fine honeymoon supper. After it was over – after the gypsy orchestra and the Governor of the state had departed – the billionaire Paddy poured two glasses of 100-year-old French liqueur for himself and his bride. But then the new lady of the house spoiled it all by saying, as the bridegroom carried her up to bed: 'Jesus Christ! This is what always happens to me when I have a couple of drinks with a guy.'

*　　*　　*

Lurching out of the tonsorial chair just after he'd had a very close and very bad shave, the customer demanded a glass of water from the Irish barber. 'Why so?' he was asked.
The answer was quick: 'Just to make sure my throat hasn't been cut.'

*　　*　　*

Q. How does a drunk qualify for membership in the Dublin branch of Alcoholics Anonymous?
A. By continuing to drink no more than two quarts of whisky a day.

* * *

Q. Please qualify the expression 'Irish virgin'.
A. Sorry, man, we can't – we just can't.

* * *

'I think you'd better take a taxi home,' the kindly old policeman advised the Irish drunk.
'I'd like to, officer,' the Irishman said, 'but my wife wouldn't let me keep it in the house.'

* * *

Listen, if you don't believe in Darwin's Law of Evolution, then how do you account for the Irish?

* * *

Q. What happens to Irish with incurable bad breath?
A. They invariably become dentists.

* * *

Stoned out of his skull on booze, Paddy jumped into a taxi and told the driver to drive around twenty times. 'And get a move on, I'm in a hurry.'

*   *   *

Sick of the terrible weather in the Windy City, Flossie the Irish streetwalker decided to move to Florida. Since then she has been immensely popular in Miami and Miami Beach. Down there in citrusland she has become famous as 'The Tail of Two Cities.'

*   *   *

'Hey,' O'Reilly said to his next door neighbour. 'I got a heavy date tonight and I'd like to borrow your car.'
'You borrowed it last night and didn't bring it back,' the neighbour said irritably.
'That's too bad,' said O'Reilly, 'I wanted to borrow it again tonight.'

*   *   *

'Why do I have to wait so long for the half broiled chicken I ordered?' the long suffering diner asked the waiter in an Irish restaurant.
'Until somebody orders the other half,' the waiter said. 'It's kind of hard to kill just half a chicken.'

*   *   *

Q. How can you tell if you've been raped by an elephant?
A. You'll be pregnant for three years.

*　　*　　*

'I see you're in here for public intoxication,' the judge told Paddy in a stern voice.
'I ain't fussy where I drink,' said the Irishman. 'Just break out the booze.'

*　　*　　*

'I wouldn't call sex such a driving force,' Paddy told a friend. 'Personally I prefer it when I'm parked somewhere.'

*　　*　　*

'How did you get that lovely mink coat?' the Irish girl asked her friend.
'The same way minks get them, honey,' was the answer she got.

*　　*　　*

'Mr. MacBain, I came here to ask for permission to marry your daughter,' Paddy started off in the presence of the Scottish-American millionaire.

'That's fine, my boy,' the old guy said. 'But I hear you drink a lot.'

'Sure I do,' answered Paddy, 'but we'll get to that later. Right now, what do you say about your daughter?'

* * *

'Money can't buy love,' O'Reilly said, 'but it can put you in a good bargaining position.'

* * *

Murphy reckons that as far as he was concerned, the perfect wife would be a beautiful, horny, deaf mute who owned a bar and restaurant.

* * *

'My wife just ran off with the nicest guy in the world,' Paddy told Mick.

'You must like him a lot, to talk about him like that,' said the other man.

'No,' said Paddy, 'I never even met the guy.'

* * *

Q. In what month of the year do Irish drink the least Guinness.
A. February.

*   *   *

She was only an Irish bookkeeper's daughter but she'd let anybody make an entry.

*   *   *

Have you heard about the Irish woodworm? It was found in a brick.

*   *   *

Have you heard about the Irishman who thought Spbruce Forsyth was a Christmas tree.

*   *   *

When an Irishman was asked what he thought about people kissing nuns, he said.
'It's alright to kiss a nun once, and it's OK to kiss a nun twice, but whatever you do you mustn't get into the habit.'

*   *   *

An Irishman was caught pouring boiling water down a rabbit hole on Good Friday, and when he was asked what he was doing, he said.
'Oh, I'm just trying to make some Hot Cross bunnies.'

*   *   *

Have you heard the Irish knock-knock joke?
'Knock Knock.'
'Who's there?'
'Olga.'
'Olga who?'
'Starsky and Hutch.'

*   *   *

An Irishman won the Tour de France last year and then went missing for three weeks doing a lap of honour.

*   *   *

Or the Irishman who drowned filling his pen in the Black Sea.

*   *   *

Why don't we get any bananas from Ireland? Because they throw away all the bent ones.

*   *   *

An Englishman and an Irishman were walking through a field when they saw a cow.
'By George, fine old English cow over there look.'
'Rubbish,' said the Irishman, 'that's a Scottish cow, you can see, it's got bagpipes underneath.'

*   *   *

Have you heard about the Irishman who lost his hat in a cow field – he had to try on 20 more before he found his own.

*   *   *

An Irishman and an Englishman were watching a film, when the Englishman said –
'I bet that cowboy falls off his horse at the end of the film.'
'OK,' said the Irishman, 'I'll put a fiver on it.'
So the Englishman agreed, and sure enough he fell off his horse at the end of the film.
'Let's have your money,' said the Englishman. 'But how come you were so sure.'
'Well, I saw it last night and he fell off, but I didn't think he'd be stupid enough to do it again tonight.'

*   *   *

Why have Irish umbrellas got holes in them?
So the Irish can see when it's raining.

*   *   *

Have you heard about the Irish pop star? He fell off the bottle.

*   *   *

An Irish turkey was talking one day when the other said. 'Cor Blimey, it's cold.'
'Yes,' said the Irish turkey, 'I'll really be glad when it's Christmas.'

*   *   *

Have you heard about the Irishman who applied for a job as a deckhand on a submarine.

*   *   *

One day a teacher asked her class what nationality Father Christmas was. When a young Irish boy put up his hand and said.
'Oh he must be from Germany because on all my presents it says "made in Hong Kong." '

*   *   *

The Irish are going to send a rocket to the moon, but unfortunately they can't find a bottle large enough.

*   *   *

A man went to a pet shop and asked the man if he had any dead hamsters.
'Why do you want those?' said the shopkeeper.
'I make jam out of them,' replied the Irishman.
'You don't eat that do you?' he said.
'No I put it on my tulips,' he said.
'Pardon, you put it on your tulips?'
'Yeh, haven't you heard? Tulips from 'amster jam.'

*　　*　　*

Have you heard of the Irish eunuch who entered himself for the No Ball Prize.

*　　*　　*

The Irish have found oil in the Irish sea, but unfortunately it is too thick to mine.

*　　*　　*

Why have the Arabs got oil and the Irish potatoes? Because the Irish had the first pick.

*　　*　　*

Have you heard of the lazy Irish tramp who volunteered as a railway sleeper.

*　　*　　*

How do you get an Irishman confused? Put him in a barrel and tell him to stand in a corner.

* * *

An Irishman was driving down the motorway when he saw a sign which said 'Clean toilets, 20 yards'. He was very pleased he'd finished because it only took him half an hour.

* * *

Have you heard of the Irish crook who turned himself in hoping to get a reward.

* * *

In 1706 the Irish invented the toilet seat, and in 1707 the English put a hole in it.

* * *

Have you heard of the Irish major who resigned after he received a letter marked private.

* * *

An Irishman was walking down the road with a cabbage on the end of a lead. When he was asked what he was doing with a cabbage on a lead, he exclaimed. 'Oh, I must have been tricked, I was told it was a collie.'

*　　*　　*

Two unemployed Irishmen were standing outside a police station when they saw a notice which said: 'one man wanted for bank robbery, three masked men wanted for murder, an old age pensioner wanted for mugging an old lady and two black men wanted for rape.'
'Cor blimey,' said one man, 'the blackies get all the good jobs around here, don't they.'

*　　*　　*

Two Irish terrorists were talking to each other on the phone.
'The shipment of guns is coming in today, Paddy.'
'What's that?' the other said.
'The guns are coming in today.'
'What's that again?'
'Look the guns are coming in today. G for Jesus, U for onions, N for knickers and S for Celtic.'

*　　*　　*

A pupil asked his Irish schoolteacher why the leaning tower of Pisa leant.
He said he didn't know but it was probably because it didn't eat.

* * *

An Irishman was eating in a bar when he found a worm in his pie.
'Waiter, there's a worm in my pie.'
'Oh, it looks like fat, sir.'
'Well, it's entitled to be isn't it, it's eating all my meat.'

All Futura Books are available at your bookshop or
newsagent, or can be ordered from the following address:
Futura Books, Cash Sales Department,
P.O. Box 11, Falmouth, Cornwall.

Please send cheque or postal order (no currency), and
allow 55p for postage and packing for the first book
plus 22p for the second book and 14p for each additional
book ordered up to a maximum charge of £1.75 in U.K.

Customers in Eire and B.F.P.O. please allow 55p for
the first book, 22p for the second book plus 14p per
copy for the next 7 books, thereafter 8p per book.

Overseas customers please allow £1 for postage and
packing for the first book and 25p per copy for each
additional book.